For everyone who stayed
indoors in 2020

First US edition 2022

Library of Congress Catalog Card Number 2021943996
ISBN 978-1-5362-1533-5

CCP 26 25 24 23 22
10 9 8 7 6 5 4 3 2

Printed in Shenzhen, Guangdong, China

This book was typeset in DIN.
The illustrations were done in mixed media.

Candlewick Studio
an imprint of
Candlewick Press
99 Dover Street
Somerville, Massachusetts 02144

www.candlewickstudio.com

CANDLEWICK STUDIO
an imprint of Candlewick Press

MY BIG BOOK OF OUTDOORS

Welcome! In every season, there is something different to see, discover, make, and do. So step outdoors and into nature!

SPRING

SUMMER

FALL

WINTER

Sunlight and warmth

Bulbs in bloom

Rain showers

New shoots growing

Birds nesting

Trees in blossom

SPRING

Signs of Spring

When spring arrives, our days become warm and light. Rain showers help grass, flowers, and trees to grow. Here are some of the first signs of spring:

Blossoms on trees
Blossoms on the branches of trees are one of spring's most spectacular sights.

Daffodils
Bright flowers burst from their bulbs. Look for daffodils; each one is like a ray of sunshine.

Twigs in beaks
Birds build their nests to make a home for their chicks.

Baby animals
Lambs are born in spring when there is plenty of fresh grass for the sheep to eat and turn into milk for their young.

3

Early Risers

Birds can sing any time of day, but early in the morning their songs are often full of life. This is known as the dawn chorus.

Song thrushes have a musical sound, with repeated notes.

Blackbirds start singing before the sun comes up.

Starlings are very good mimics. They can copy the sounds of other birds—and even human speech.

Skylarks are known for their song flight. They hover in the air singing a warbling song.

Nightingales are famous for their beautiful lilting song.

Wrens are very loud and can sing two notes at the same time.

5

Home Grown

At the start of spring, birds collect
twigs, leaves, and moss to build their nests.
The nest is a safe place for birds to lay
their eggs and store food.

You will need:
3.5 oz of chocolate
1 cup of shredded wheat, crushed
6 cupcake liners
18 small chocolate eggs

Chocolate Nests

1. Ask an adult to melt the chocolate in a bowl, then stir in the crushed shredded wheat.

2. Spoon the mix into cupcake liners and press a teaspoon in the center to make a nest shape.

3. Add three chocolate eggs to each nest. Pop the nests in the fridge until they are set.

7

Round and Strong

Eggs come in lots of shapes and sizes, but all have a tough outer shell, which may be colorful or speckled.

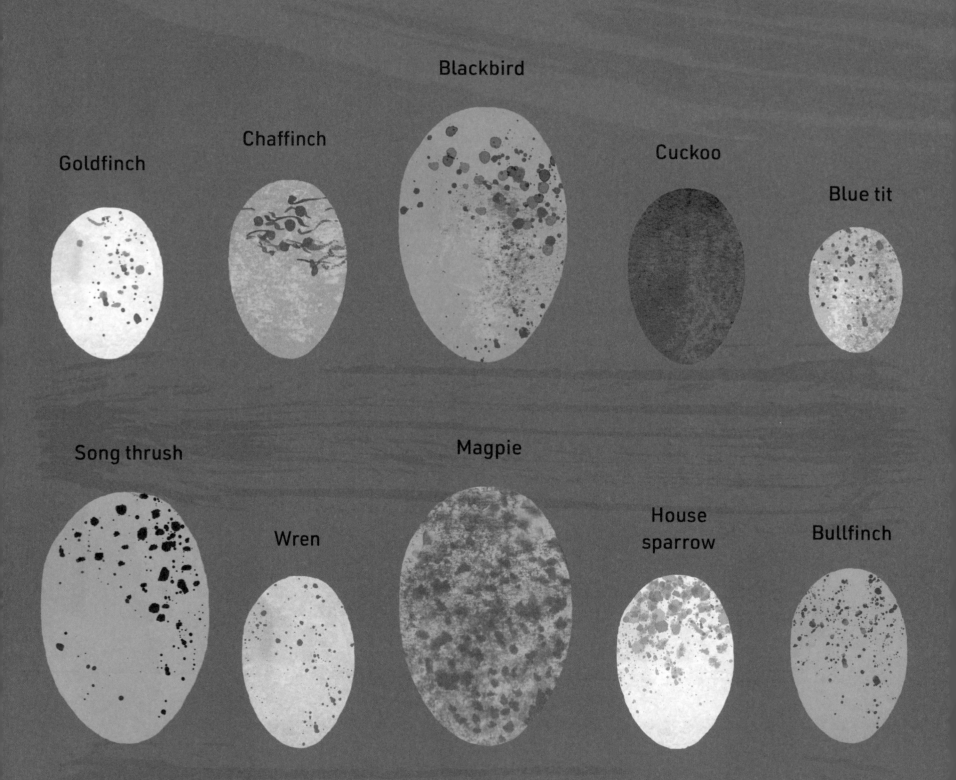

Goldfinch

Chaffinch

Blackbird

Cuckoo

Blue tit

Song thrush

Wren

Magpie

House sparrow

Bullfinch

Light and Fluffy

Feathers give birds their color, keep them warm, and allow them to fly. Most birds have ten flight feathers on each wing. If these feathers are lost, the bird cannot fly.

Goldfinch

Tawny owl

Magpie

Wood pigeon

Cool Places

Stones block out wind and
sunshine and keep the ground
cool, dark, and damp—the
perfect place for insects to
live. Insects with hard shells
can push under stones to find
food and shelter.

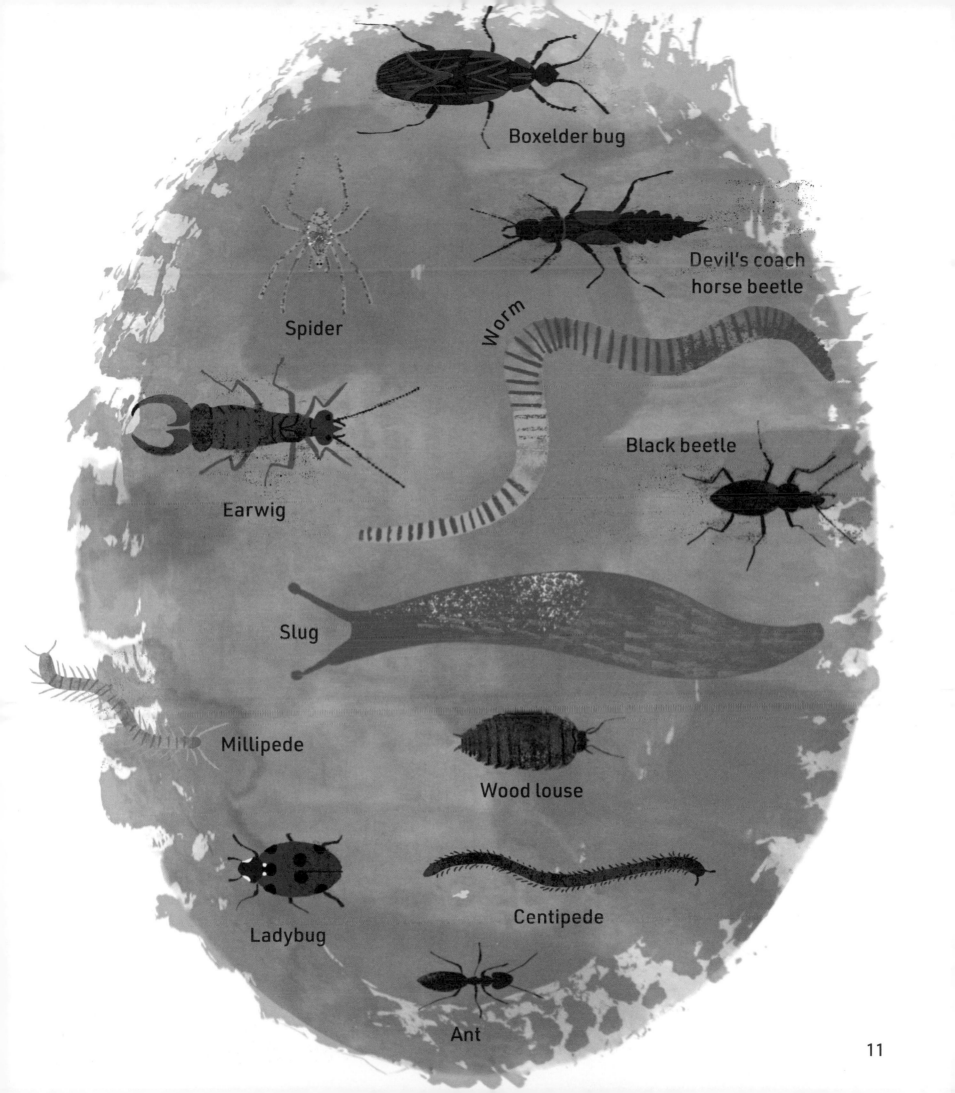

Boxelder bug

Devil's coach
horse beetle

Spider

Worm

Earwig

Black beetle

Slug

Millipede

Wood louse

Ladybug

Centipede

Ant

Bug Hotel

Get outdoors and make the perfect home for beetles, bugs, and creatures of all kinds!

You will need:
2-3 recycled wooden pallets
Twine
Natural or recycled materials

1. Choose a cool, shady spot and ask an adult to check that the ground is stable.

2. Ask an adult to create the structure by stacking the pallets on top of each other and securing them in place with twine.

3. Now it's time to fill in the gaps of the pallets with natural or recycled materials to attract bugs to the hotel!

Bark is a great shelter for beetles, spiders, and millipedes.

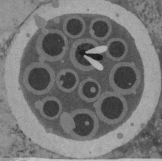

Hollow stems such as bamboo are ideal places for solitary bees to lay their eggs.

Dry leaves provide homes for ladybugs when it gets colder.

Broken plant pots make great shady
spaces for frogs and newts.

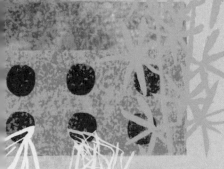

Corrugated
cardboard
can be rolled
up tightly
to attract
lacewings.

Hay and straw
give insects a
good place to burrow
and hibernate.

Deadwood can make a great
home for burrowing centipedes
and wood lice.

Underground Home

Ants live in big groups called colonies where they all have different jobs to do.

Princess ants take flight after the summer rains and go in search of a suitable place to lay their eggs.

Soldier ants are strong ants that protect the colony. Their super-strength helps them to carry objects far larger than themselves.

Worker ants are the smallest ants in the colony. They find food, care for larvae, and help build the nest.

Drone ants are the only male ants living in the colony. Only drone ants and princess ants have wings. They take flight once a year to mate. A princess ant becomes a queen ant when she establishes her own colony.

The queen is the founder of the colony and can lay thousands of eggs each day. When a queen ant finds a suitable home for her colony, she will eat her wings, as she no longer needs them.

15

Super Soil

Soil is important for every living thing. Plants anchor themselves in it and use its nutrients to make food. Water passing through the soil is filtered and cleaned. Soil also absorbs and releases gases that help clean our air.

Wriggling worms help to improve the soil. As they burrow deep into the earth, they loosen the soil, which allows water to soak in and helps plants to grow.

Below Ground

The top layer of soil is made up of dead plants and animal waste.

The middle layer is hard and sandy.

The bottom layer is rock.

Growing Green

Spring is the ideal time for most plants to grow.
Warmth from the sun, long days full of light,
and frequent rain showers provide the perfect
conditions for plants to grow
bigger and stronger.

Growing a Cress Head

1. Wet small pieces of paper towel and put them in the bottom of each eggshell.

2. Wet some cotton balls and carefully place them on top of the paper towel, making sure there is a gap between the cotton balls and the top of the eggshell.

3. Sprinkle some cress seeds on top of the cotton balls and gently press them down.

4. Leave your eggshells in a sunny spot indoors and water gently once a day. Watch the cress hair grow!

You will need:
Eggshells
Paper towels
Cotton balls
Cress seeds

Splish Splash!

Plip

plop

plip-plip-plop

pitter-patter

pitter-patter

drip, drop

splash!

Pitter-patter

pitter-patter

drip, drop

splash!

Drip-drop

drip-drop

drip

drip

stop!

Spring Bulbs

Flowers grown from bulbs appear in spring year after year. They are one of nature's most lovely surprises!

Hyacinth

Iris

Bluebell

Tulip

Daffodil

Crocus

23

Frog Spawn to Frog!

Tiny eggs float on water in a jelly mass.

A tadpole hatches and swims.

It grows two hind legs.

Soon it has four legs and the tail starts to disappear.

Now it's a frog. Croak! Croak!

24

Is It a Frog or a Toad?

While frogs have moist, smooth skin and spend most of their time in or near water, toads have dry, rough skin and spend most of their time on land.

This is a toad.

Pond Dipping

You will need:
A nearby pond (always with an adult)
A net
A flat tray

1. Ask an adult to help you swish your net in the pond, then carefully turn it out in the tray.

2. Can you spot any plants or tiny creatures in the tray? Can you name them?

3. When you've finished your pond dip, ask an adult to gently empty the tray back into the pond.

Pond snail

Tadpoles

Water beetle larva

Water beetle

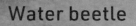

Water mite

Water spider

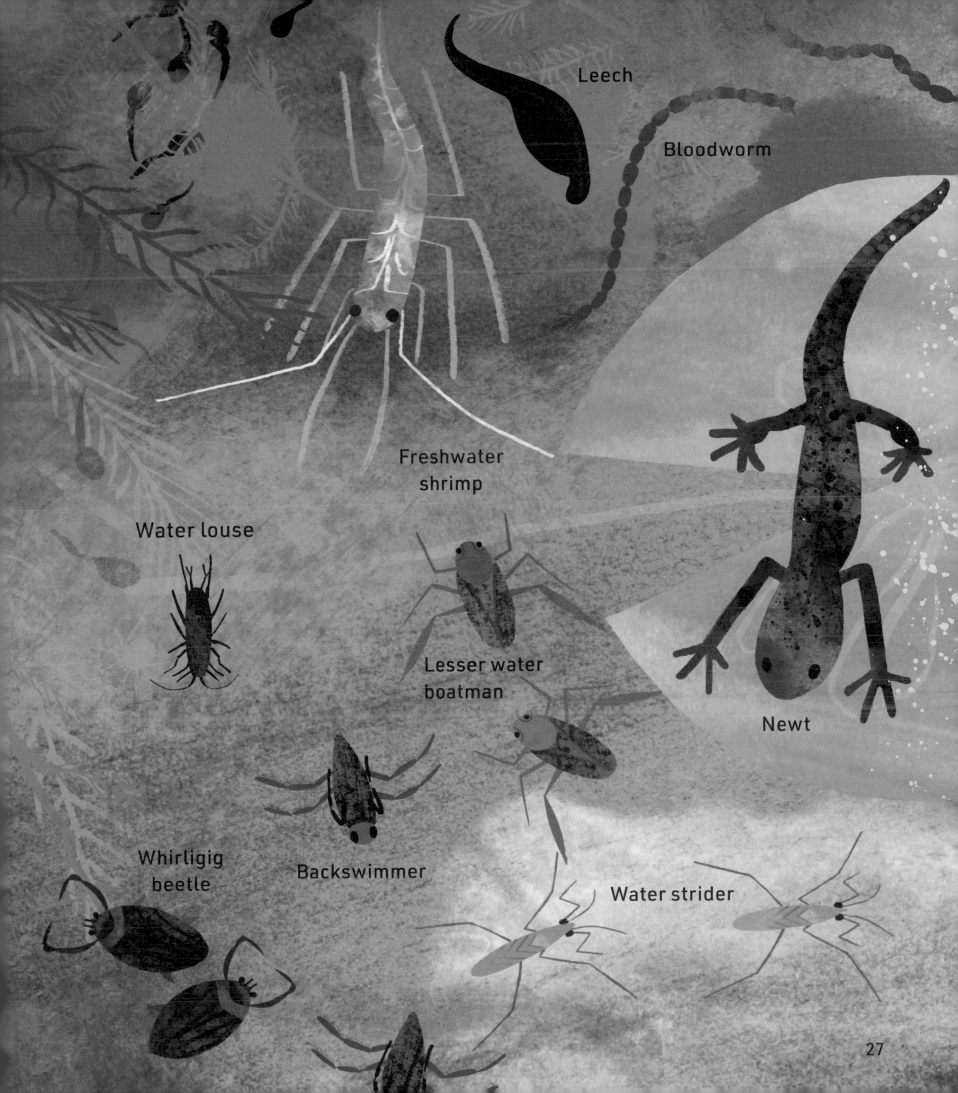

Leech

Bloodworm

Freshwater
shrimp

Water louse

Lesser water
boatman

Newt

Whirligig
beetle

Backswimmer

Water strider

27

Rainbow, Rainbow

Rainbow, rainbow, vivid and bright

Always such a fabulous sight

Rainbow, rainbow, fading away

Come back and see us on another wet day

Sunny play

Umbrella shade

More of the day

Insects everywhere

Sweet-smelling flowers

Ripe and juicy berries

SUMMER

Signs of Summer

Summer days are brighter and warmer than any other season. Here are some of the first signs of summer:

Insects arrive
More and more insects can be spotted flying around.

Flowers bloom
Bright-colored flowers open up in the warm sunshine.

First flight
Baby birds leave the
nest to make their first flight.

Bright sunshine
The sun rises earlier and the days are longer.

Harvest time
Colorful fruits and
vegetables begin
to ripen and are
ready to eat.

33

Insects Everywhere

How many of these flying insects have you seen?

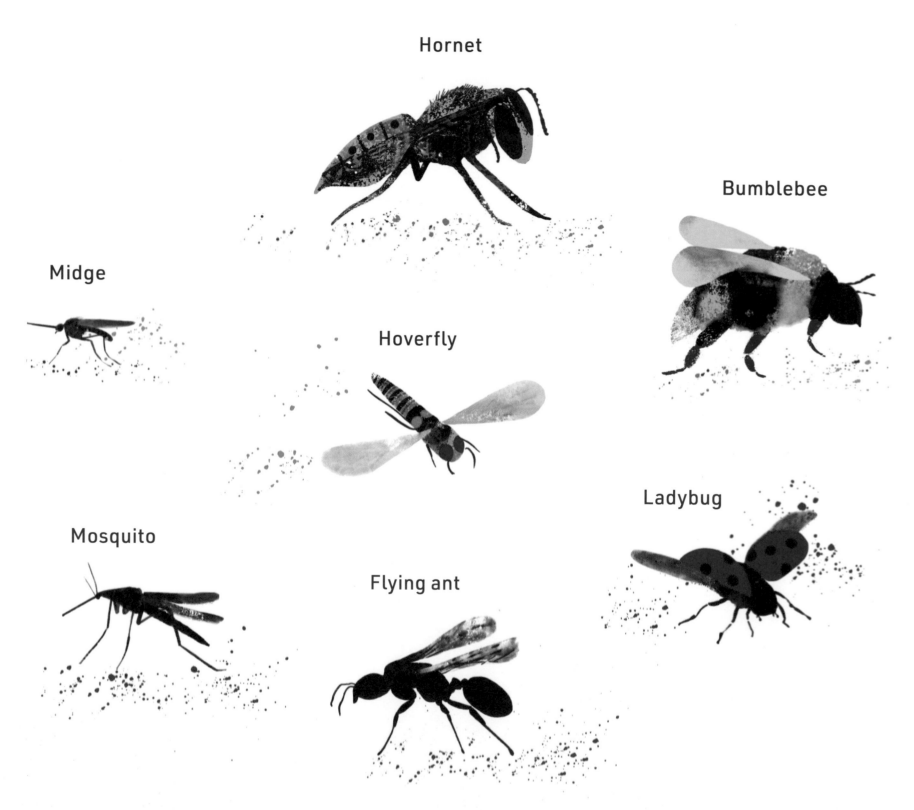

Hornet

Bumblebee

Midge

Hoverfly

Ladybug

Mosquito

Flying ant

Dragonfly

Bluebottle fly

Mayfly

Horsefly

Garden tiger moth

Wasp

Stag beetle

Crane fly

Tiny Egg to Butterfly!

Inside an egg a tiny caterpillar grows.

The caterpillar hatches and starts to eat and grow.

When fully grown, the caterpillar stops eating and becomes a pupa.

Then the butterfly emerges!

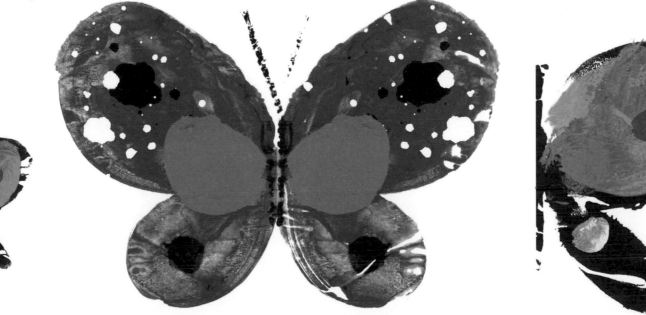

Paint
a Butterfly

1. Fold a piece of paper in half and open it up again.

2. Paint two wing patterns on one side of the fold line, then press the paper back together.

3. Open it up to reveal a butterfly with matching wings.

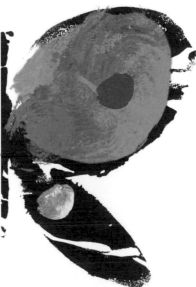

Beautiful Butterflies

Butterflies can be many different shapes and their patterns come in all sorts of colors. Here are some of my favorites:

Red admirals
fly to warmer places
when it gets cold.

Monarchs
flap their wings ten
times a second.

Silverspots
are an endangered species.

Brimstone
wings look a lot
like leaves.

Peacock
butterfly wings have "eyes"
like peacock feathers.

Orange-barred sulphurs
are found in the Americas
and the Caribbean.

Malachites
start out as horned,
prickly black caterpillars
with red spotted
markings.

Common blues
like to live in sunny,
sheltered spots.

Busy Bees

Honey bees
live in large hives. There are lots of worker bees but only one queen bee. Each bee has a different role to play.

Worker bees collect pollen and nectar to feed the colony.

Drone bees are male and their job is to mate with the queen. They have big eyes and large, powerful wings.

The queen bee is essential to life in the hive.

Flower Power

Flowers attract bees and other insects, big and small, that spread their pollen to make even more flowers. This is called pollination. We need to protect bees to help flowers and other plants to grow on our planet.

Dandelion Clocks

Some flowers are pollinated by the wind. Seeds are blown far and wide to make new flowers.

A whisper of wind is all it takes

For a meadow of stems to sway

And then all at once

With just one puff

The tiny seeds drift away

Grow a Sunflower

Isn't it amazing what can grow from a tiny seed?

Put a sunflower seed in a pot and cover it with soil.

Place it in a sunny spot and water it a little every day.

Now watch it grow, grow, grow.

Daisies Everywhere

Daisies can be
found growing nearly
everywhere in the world.
Other names for daisies
include goose flower,
herb Margaret,
bruisewort, and
noon flower.

Make a little hole at the bottom of a daisy stalk. Thread another daisy stalk through the hole and pull it through. Keep going until you get a long **daisy chain.**

47

Summer Color

In the warmth of the sun, fruit and vegetables ripen. Soon they will be ready for picking. All around there is glorious color. Watch as strawberries turn from pale green to deep, deep red.

Cherries

Black currants

Raspberries

Gooseberries

Strawberries

Tomatoes

Peas

Corn

Chilies

Summer Nights

And in those final moments of daylight

All the beauty of the world was

   reflected in the sky

Full of hope

Full of wonder

I looked forward to another day

Another day of holiday!

Buckets of Fun

Tide pools are shallow pools of water found on a beach. What can you find in a tide pool?

Brittle starfish

Dog whelk

Starfish

Sea anemone

Limpets

Mussels

Green crab

Pipefish

Blenny

Hermit crab

Mermaid's purse

Seaweed

Shell Spotter

All shells once had small creatures living inside of them—some still do! How many of these shells have you seen on the shore?

Queen scallop

Mussel

Tower shell

Common periwinkle

Angel wing

Common whelk

Common limpet

Common cockle

Sunray venus

Dog whelk

Painted topshell

Spotted cowrie

Florida horse conch

Razor shell

Stormy Weather

When thunder and lightning happen at the
same time, the storm is directly overhead.

Dark clouds

Lightning flash

Silence, then . . .

Thunderclap

Misty mornings

Leaves falling

Blustery winds

Birds migrating

Acorns on the ground

Gathering the crops

FALL

Signs of Fall

Autumn, or fall, is cool, windy, and sometimes wet. The days become shorter, and night comes earlier. Here are some of the first signs of fall:

Taking flight
Some birds fly off to warmer places. You may see them flying together in a V formation, with one bird leading the way.

Blowing around
The wind is usually a bit stronger in fall. Can you spot any leaves blowing in the wind?

Changing color
Trees once filled with green leaves are now full of orange, yellow, and red leaves.

Forest foraging
Squirrels collect nuts that have ripened and fallen to the ground. Look out for acorns, chestnuts, and hazelnuts.

Under your feet
As leaves dry out, they fall from the trees. Can you hear them crunching under your feet?

Leaf Litter

Trees can be identified by the shape of their leaves. In autumn, they fall from the trees and create leaf litter. Have you found any of these common leaf shapes on the ground?

Willow

Oak

Birch

Elm

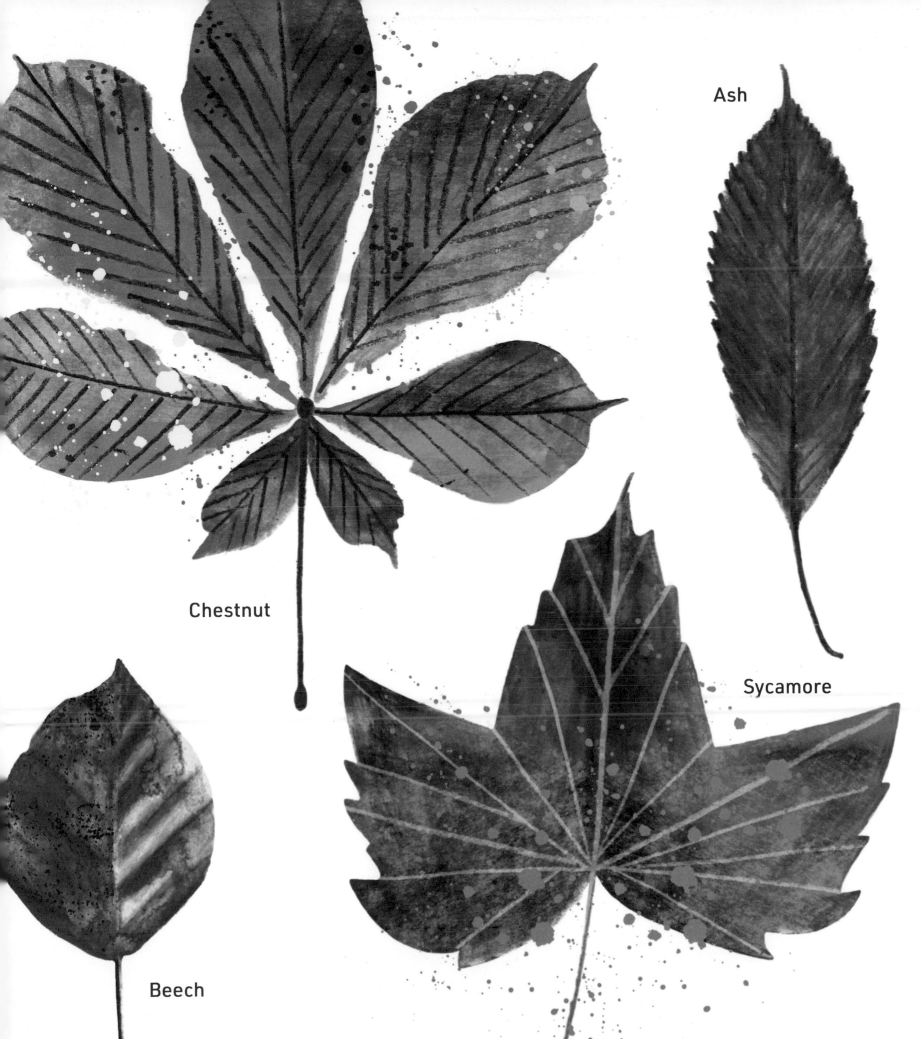

Ash

Chestnut

Sycamore

Beech

63

Changing Colors

When fall comes, it's time for trees to get ready for winter. Trees send food from the green leaves down to the roots. The leaves then turn yellow, orange, red, or brown before falling to the ground.

Leaf Mobile

You will need:
Two sticks
Fall leaves
String

1. Find two sticks. Make a cross shape and tie the sticks together with string.

2. Collect fall leaves from the ground and make a little hole in the stem of each leaf.

3. Feed some string through each stem and secure with a small knot. Repeat this until you have 6-10 strings of leaves, making sure each length of string is different.

4. Attach the other end of each string to the cross shape and hang your mobile up.

On a Day Like Today

Precious seeds

Carried by the wind

On a day like today

Sent spiraling around and around

May one day grow to be

MIGHTY trees

Scattering seeds

Carried by the wind

On a day just like today

Carried by the Wind

Trees need to send their seeds far and wide to take root and grow in different places.

Some tree seeds have wings to help them fly. They glide, whirl, and spin in the wind that carries them to their new homes.

The Forest

In autumn, the forest is full of life as fungi and fallen leaves appear and animals prepare for winter. What can you see in the forest?

Squirrels

Squirrels make their dens in the trunks of trees or build nests in branches out of twigs and leaves.

Squirrels use their bushy tails to protect themselves from the weather, to balance when they climb, and to communicate with one another.

Squirrels like to eat nuts, fruits, and seeds. During fall, they hide their food, burying it in the soft earth to eat over the winter months.

From Tall Oaks, Little Acorns Grow

A tiny acorn can grow into a giant oak tree that can live for hundreds of years. Isn't that amazing?

Acorns grow throughout the summer, then fall to the ground in autumn when they are fully grown.

Squirrels and other animals scatter them around the forest—some of these acorns turn into new trees!

The acorn splits open, then grows a shoot and roots. The seedling will grow and grow until it turns into a small tree.

The new tree grows taller and eventually another little acorn appears.

73

Beach plums

Huckleberries

Elderberries

Blackberries

Foraging for Fruit

There are lots of colorful fruits to spot growing
on trees and bushes in the fall.

Pears

Damsons

Quinces

Rose hips

Plums

75

Gala

Golden Delicious

Granny Smith

Pink Lady

McIntosh

Taste an Apple

Apple trees take four to five years to produce their first fruit. The trees can live for 100 years. There are more than 8,000 types of apple. How many have you tasted?

Fuji

Jazz

Empire

Braeburn

Bramley

Bake this apple before tasting!

Honeycrisp

Bake an Apple

1. Ask an adult to help you wash and core an apple.

2. Fill the core with raisins or berries, a little sugar or honey, and a touch of cinnamon.

3. Bake in the oven at 350°F (180°C) for 20 minutes until soft and serve with ice cream.

Where Are These Birds Flying To?

Starlings
from eastern Europe fly to the UK in search of food. It's thought that nearly a million starlings spend winter there.

Swallows
migrate from the UK to South Africa for the winter. This journey takes up to six weeks. They eat flying insects on the way!

As the days become shorter, many birds fly off in search of warmer weather. This is known as migration. Some birds fly much farther than others.

Swifts
spend winter in Africa, south of the Sahara, where they follow the rains to find the best food to eat.

Cuckoos
fly south from the UK to central Africa for winter. They stop to rest and feed along the way.

Flying together in formation means that no bird gets left behind.

Flying behind one another stops them from getting too tired on their long journey.

Sky Shapes

Some birds, like geese, can be seen flying in a V-shaped formation in the sky during the fall.

The birds take turns flying at the front.

The airflow from the bird ahead allows them to glide more easily.

Cirrocumulus clouds look like ripples of water on a lake. They are a sign of fair weather.

Altocumulus clouds are a mix

Cumulus clouds are large, white, fluffy clouds that appear on sunny days.

Clouds

Fall weather can change from moment to moment. Watch the clouds to see if you can predict the weather.

Cirrus clouds are thin, wispy clouds floating very high in the sky in fair weather.

water and ice found in calm weather.

Stratus clouds are wavy clouds floating low in the sky, often a sign of light rain.

Nimbostratus clouds are low, flat, dark clouds, usually a sign of continuous rain, snow, or sleet.

Harvest Moon

The harvest moon is
big and bright

It rises early as the
sun goes down

And glows like a lantern
all through the night

As the farmers
harvest the land

Gathering the crops
in time for winter

In the light of the
harvest moon

White and still

Icy ponds

Nighttime skies

Tracks in snow

Everything quiet

Animals in hibernation

WINTER

Clear night skies make the stars appear much brighter and easier to see.

Signs of Winter

Winter is the coldest season. As the temperature drops, the chilly weather brings frost, ice, and sometimes even snow! Here are some of the first signs of winter:

Bright berries
Birds feed on berries throughout winter when other food is hard to find.

Foggy mornings

Fog can form early in the winter mornings before the sun rises or late in the afternoon as the sun goes down.

Freezing over

Look out for ice on lakes and ponds and icicles hanging from roofs and tree branches.

Frosty chill

Morning frost appears on cobwebs, bushes, and trees.

Robins are quite friendly around people and may come close if you are quiet.

Robin Redbreast

Not all birds fly off to warmer places in winter; some birds stay at home. Robins can survive the cold by fluffing up their feathers. Air trapped between the layers of their feathers helps keep them warm even on the chilliest of days.

Beautiful Birds

Here are four of my favorite cold-weather birds.
What birds do you spot in the winter?

Great spotted
woodpecker

Yellowhammer

Blue tit

Magpie

Make a Bird Feeder

It can be hard for birds to find food in the winter. Make this simple feeder and hang it in your garden.

You will need:
Birdseed
A tray
Honey
An empty toilet
  paper roll
String

1. Tip some birdseed into a tray.

2. Gently squeeze honey over the toilet paper roll. Roll the tube in the seeds and leave it to dry.

3. Thread some string through the tube and ask an adult to hang the feeder outside. Watch and see what birds come to feed!

Silent Searches

Silently searching
Cutting through the sky
Back and forth
Listening for movement
A shiver is all it takes

Silently swooping
Diving through the dark
Talons capture with precision
Breaking the silence
On a cold winter's night

Who Has Been Here?

Different types of animals leave different footprints in the snow. Next time it snows, see if you can figure out who has been walking in the snow before you!

Rabbits' hind feet are much larger than their front feet, so watch out for a pair of long prints and a pair of shorter prints.

Deer hooves leave two long prints in the snow with a gap in between.

Fox paws have two toes at the front, one toe on each side, and a chevron-shaped pad at the back. Look out for claw marks!

Long and thin, **bird tracks** often look like arrows.

Cats have four toes on each paw. Their hind feet land in their front tracks when they walk.

Squirrels have four front toes and five skinny hind toes. If the tracks are clear, you may see their claw marks.

Snug and Warm

To survive the cold of winter, when it is harder to find food,
some creatures go into a very deep sleep called hibernation.

Dormice
These small
creatures typically
nest in brambles or
beneath piles of leaves
on the forest floor.

Hedgehogs
These spiny
mammals eat as
much as possible
during fall and then
look for a quiet place
to spend the winter
months to save their
energy.

Snowdrops

Snowdrops are a sign
that winter is nearly over.
On warmer winter days
snowdrops open up their outer
petals to reveal the nectar inside.

If the weather is too cold, the petals close up and protect the nectar inside.

Snowdrop nectar is an important food for bees.

Evergreen Forest

Evergreen trees keep their leaves all year round.
Most conifers are evergreen and have downward-
sloping branches—this helps snow to slide off easily
and stops the tree from freezing.

Cedar

Douglas fir

Conifers

The thin, pointy leaves on conifer trees are called needles. Here are some different types of conifers. How many can you spot?

Yew

Larch

Scots pine

Clever Cones

Different types of pine trees have differently shaped pine cones. The woody cones have individual "scales" and are used to keep the seeds of the tree safe and dry. The pine cones open up in warm, dry weather to release the seeds so they can grow.

Pine Cone Weather Station

Collect fallen pine cones and place them on a windowsill. Notice how on a fine, dry day the cones will open up. But if it's going to rain, they start to close. How clever is that!

Limber

Loblolly

Longleaf

Slash

Scots

Shortleaf

Pinyon

Oh, I Wish It Would Snow

Oh, I wish it would snow
Just once, just for me

Oh, I wish that tomorrow when I wake up
There's a white brightness waiting behind the curtains
And when I look out I see nothing but
Snow, snow, snow

So much snow
It's billowing off the rooftops

So much snow
It's swept up over the hedges

So much snow
We can throw snowballs, go sledding,
And build a snowman
That stays for days and days!

Oh, I wish it would snow

How Is Snow Made?

Snowflakes are made inside clouds when water droplets freeze and turn into ice crystals.

The ice crystals get bigger and bigger as they attract water vapor from the surrounding air before falling as snowflakes to earth.

Snowflakes that fall through freezing, dry air are needle- or rod-shaped. They produce snow that is fine and powdery.

Snowflakes that fall through moist air will melt at the edges and stick together. These flakes are big and delicate; they are perfect for making snowballs!

How to Make a

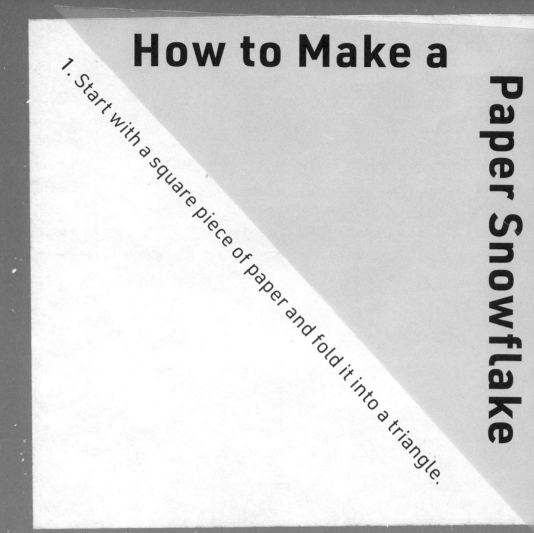

1. Start with a square piece of paper and fold it into a triangle.

2. Fold the triangle in half again to make a smaller triangle.

3. With the center point of the triangle facing toward you, fold the right-hand side slightly past the middle. Now fold the left-hand side over so that its outer edge lines up with the outer edge of the right side.

110

4. Flip the shape over and you will see a horizontal fold.

5. Using scissors, cut a semicircle below the horizontal fold.

6. Cut straight or curvy lines into the edges of your folded triangle.

7. Unfold to reveal your snowflake in all its glory!

The Little Dipper looks like a small ladle. The bright star on the end of the Little Dipper is the North Star, Polaris. If you were standing at the North Pole, Polaris would be directly above you.

The Big Dipper is made up of seven bright stars and is one of the easiest constellations to spot in the Northern Hemisphere.

Star Shapes

A constellation is a cluster of stars that creates an imaginary shape, like a connect-the-dots in the night sky. In the past, these connections between the brightest stars helped people navigate ships as they sailed across oceans.

Orion (also known as
the Hunter) is one of the
brightest constellations
in the night sky and can be
seen around the world. Look
for three equally bright stars in
a short row; these are known as
Orion's Belt because they are found
across the middle of Orion.

Phases of the Moon

As the moon travels around the earth, it is lit by the sun. The different phases of the moon show us where it is on its journey. It takes the moon about one month to orbit the earth.

New Moon   Waxing Crescent    First Quarter    Waxing Gibbous

NORTHERN HEMISPHERE

New Moon    Waxing Crescent   First Quarter    Waxing Gibbous

SOUTHERN HEMISPHERE

The phases of the moon look different depending on whether
you are in the Southern or Northern Hemisphere.

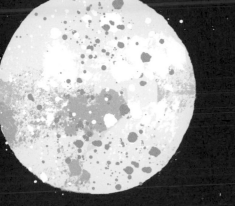  

Full Moon   Waning Gibbous   Third Quarter   Waning Crescent

Full Moon   Waning Gibbous   Third Quarter   Waning Crescent

Looking Up

I should be asleep, but I'm not
Instead I'm gazing out of my window
I'm looking UP in wonder
And the more I look, the more I see

Star after star, after star
And even more stars

I pick one, I fix my gaze on it
Without blinking for as long as I can
My star sees me and twinkles back at me
And suddenly all there is in the universe
    is ME and MY star